LEADERSHIP PRACTICES INVENTORY

LPI

Third Edition

PARTICIPANT'S WORKBOOK

10 Steps to Understanding and Using Your LPI Feedback

JAMES M. KOUZES

BARRY Z. POSNER

Pfeiffer

A Wiley Imprint

www.pfeiffer.com

Published by Pfeiffer
An Imprint of John Wiley & Sons, Inc.

...d in any
...erwise,
...ithout
...sion should
...loboken,

...rectly

Pfeiffer also publishes its books in a variety of electronic formats. Some content that appears in print may not be available in electronic books.

ISBN: 0-7879-6726-2

Acquiring Editor: *Lisa Shannon*
Director of Development: *Kathleen Dolan Davies*
Developmental Editor: *Janis Chan*
Editor: *Rebecca Taff*
Senior Production Editor: *Dawn Kilgore*
Manufacturing Supervisor: *Bill Matherly*
Interior Design: *Yvo*

Printed in the United States of America

Printing   10 9 8 7 6 5 4 3 2 1

CONTENTS

INTRODUCTION

Make the Most of Your LPI Feedback

Those who are the best at leading are also the best at learning. Exemplary leaders don't rest on their laurels or rely on their natural talents. Whatever their individual learning styles may be, they continually do more to improve themselves.

If you want to be the best you can be, you need to become a great learner. Here are some tips on how you can get the most learning out of the LPI process.

1. LOOK FOR MESSAGES, NOT MEASURES. There's a lot of data in your LPI Feedback Report. You may be getting feedback from your manager, your direct reports, your peers, and others with whom you interact. In fact, there are likely to be more than three hundred separate numbers on the report. It's easy to get lost in all those details. Don't let the data overwhelm you. Focus on the messages, not the measures. Constantly ask yourself, "What are people trying to tell me about my leadership behavior?" "Where do I see consistencies and inconsistencies in the data?" "Where are there patterns that shape how others see my leadership?" Treat the LPI feedback not as a report card, but as valid and useful information that will help you improve.

2. ACCEPT FEEDBACK AS A GIFT. Feedback may not come wrapped in a package tied with a bow, but it's still a gift, perhaps one of the most valuable gifts you'll ever receive. Why? Because we know from our research that leaders who are the most open to feedback are far more effective than leaders who resist hearing other people's perspectives on their behaviors.

3. TAKE THE FEEDBACK SERIOUSLY. People often wonder, "Will it really make a difference if I increase the frequency of the behaviors

1

measured by the LPI?" Our research—and that of others who have used our instrument—consistently show the same results: The more frequently you demonstrate the behaviors included in the LPI, the more likely you will be seen as an effective leader.

4. TRUST THE FEEDBACK. When we were developing the LPI, we conducted a number of tests to determine whether the instrument had sound psychometric properties. Our tests confirmed that the LPI is internally reliable. This means that the six statements pertaining to each leadership Practice are highly correlated with one another.

Test/re-test reliability is also high. This means that scores from one administration of the LPI to another within a short time span (a few days or even months) and without any significant intervening event (such as a leadership training program) are consistent and stable.

The Five Practices of Exemplary Leadership® are generally independent of each other. They each measure different types of behavior, not the same behaviors.

The LPI has both face validity and predictive validity. "Face validity" means that the results make sense to people. "Predictive validity" means that the results are significantly correlated with various performance measures and can be used to make predictions about leadership effectiveness.

5. VALUE THE DIFFERENCES IN YOUR OBSERVERS' PERSPECTIVES. You're a three-dimensional person, and your feedback ought to be three-dimensional as well. You work with people from a variety of backgrounds and from a variety of functions and organizations. Information from these multiple perspectives better enables you to see how you lead across groups and situations. Value what each of your observers has to say because each gives you a bit more of a complete picture of yourself.

6. PLAN NOW TO RE-ADMINISTER. Great leaders set goals and seek feedback. The LPI gives you a snapshot in time. It is a beginning point from which to move forward. It gives you great feedback, new ideas, and a focus to lead in more effective ways. To heighten your focus and practice with great purpose, decide now that you will re-administer the instrument within a specific period of time—we recommend between six and nine months. Work with a coach, facilitator, or trainer to help determine the best time to re-administer.

STEP 1

Examine Your First Impressions

When you first looked at your LPI feedback, what was your immediate reaction? Check any of the words in the list below that express what you felt. Use the blank lines to write any other feelings you had.

❑ Amused   ❑ Pleased

❑ Challenged   ❑ Relieved

❑ Confused   ❑ Surprised

❑ Disappointed   ❑ Upset

❑ Humbled   ❑ Neutral—no strong feelings

Other: _____

Other: _____

Other: _____

Now list your *strongest* feeling and identify the primary reason you feel that way.

_____

_____

_____

STEP 2

Explore Consistency

Consistency in behavior is important to your personal credibility. It lets others know that they can count on you to be congruent in your actions from one time to the next and from one person or group to the next. They know what to expect from you.

- Do you rate yourself higher than, lower than, or about the same as others rate you? In other words, how consistent are your Self ratings with those of your Observers' ratings? Check the appropriate boxes below.

Self compared to Manager?

❏ Very consistent ❏ Somewhat consistent ❏ Not consistent

Self compared to Direct Reports?

❏ Very consistent ❏ Somewhat consistent ❏ Not consistent

Self compared to Co-Workers?

❏ Very consistent ❏ Somewhat consistent ❏ Not consistent

Self compared to Other Observers?

❏ Very consistent ❏ Somewhat consistent ❏ Not consistent

- How consistent are the responses across Observer groups?

  Manager compared to Other Observer groups?

  ❑ Very consistent ❑ Somewhat consistent ❑ Not consistent

  Direct Reports compared to Others?

  ❑ Very consistent ❑ Somewhat consistent ❑ Not consistent

  Co-Workers compared to Others?

  ❑ Very consistent ❑ Somewhat consistent ❑ Not consistent

  All Other Observers?

  ❑ Very consistent ❑ Somewhat consistent ❑ Not consistent

- How consistent are the responses within Observer groups?

  Among all Direct Reports?

  ❑ Very consistent ❑ Somewhat consistent ❑ Not consistent

  Among all Co-Workers?

  ❑ Very consistent ❑ Somewhat consistent ❑ Not consistent

  Among all Other Observers?

  ❑ Very consistent ❑ Somewhat consistent ❑ Not consistent

There are a number of valid explanations for inconsistency in your feedback. For instance, some people know you better because they interact with you more often. Different people are in different functions with different needs. It may also be that you actually behave differently toward different people because you think they need to be treated differently when in fact they do not. What's important is that you understand why people rate you differently and that you determine the extent to which you need to be consistent.

- How do you explain any inconsistencies in the feedback you're getting?

_____

_____

_____

_____

_____

_____

_____

_____

_____

_____

_____

_____

_____

_____

_____

_____

_____

_____

_____

STEP 3

Find Patterns and Listen for Messages

Any data, whether from the LPI or from another source, is only numbers or words until you can make sense of it and turn it into useful information. When you look at an impressionist painting from a few inches away, for instance, it's not much more than colored dots; it's only when you stand back that a pattern appears.

Stand back from your data and see what emerges. What patterns do you see? What messages does the data give you?

First, Look at the Leadership Behaviors Ranking

On the Leadership Behaviors Ranking page of your LPI Feedback Report, find the three to five items on which you were rated most highly by your Observers (your strengths). On the list of Leadership Behaviors Organized by Practice following this page, put a plus sign (+) next to those items. Then find the three to five items that were rated the lowest. Those are the behaviors in which you most likely need the most improvement. Put a minus sign (−) next to those items.

- Looking at the behaviors marked with a (+), what strengths are revealed? What Practices or specific behaviors do you and Observers agree you do most frequently? Are there any patterns to the items among the *top ten* on the Leadership Behaviors Ranking?

_____

_____

_____

_____

_____

_____

_____

- Looking at the behaviors marked with a (−), what areas of development are apparent? What Practices or specific behaviors do you and Observers agree you do least frequently? Are there any patterns to the items among the *bottom ten* on the Leadership Behavior Rankings?

_____

_____

_____

_____

_____

_____

_____

LEADERSHIP BEHAVIORS ORGANIZED BY PRACTICE

Model the Way

_____ **1.** I set a personal example of what I expect of others.

_____ **6.** I spend time and energy making certain that the people I work with adhere to the principles and standards we have agreed on.

_____ **11.** I follow through on the promises and commitments that I make.

_____ **16.** I ask for feedback on how my actions affect other people's performance.

_____ **21.** I build consensus around a common set of values for running our organization.

_____ **26.** I am clear about my philosophy of leadership.

Inspire a Shared Vision

_____ **2.** I talk about future trends that will influence how our work gets done.

_____ **7.** I describe a compelling image of what our future could be like.

_____ **12.** I appeal to others to share an exciting dream of the future.

_____ **17.** I show others how their long-term interests can be realized by enlisting in a common vision.

_____ **22.** I paint the "big picture" of what we aspire to accomplish.

_____ **27.** I speak with genuine conviction about the higher meaning and purpose of our work.

Challenge the Process

_____ **3.** I seek out challenging opportunities that test my own skills and abilities.

_____ 8. I challenge people to try out new and innovative ways to do their work.

_____ 13. I search outside the formal boundaries of my organization for innovative ways to improve what we do.

_____ 18. I ask "What can we learn?" when things don't go as expected.

_____ 23. I make certain that we set achievable goals, make concrete plans, and establish measurable milestones for the projects and programs that we work on.

_____ 28. I experiment and take risks, even when there is a chance of failure.

Enable Others to Act

_____ 4. I develop cooperative relationships among the people I work with.

_____ 9. I actively listen to diverse points of view.

_____ 14. I treat others with dignity and respect.

_____ 19. I support the decisions that people make on their own.

_____ 24. I give people a great deal of freedom and choice in deciding how to do their work.

_____ 29. I ensure that people grow in their jobs by learning new skills and developing themselves.

Encourage the Heart

_____ 5. I praise people for a job well done.

_____ 10. I make it a point to let people know about my confidence in their abilities.

_____ 15. I make sure that people are creatively rewarded for their contributions to the success of our projects.

_____ 20. I publicly recognize people who exemplify commitment to shared values.

_____ 25. I find ways to celebrate accomplishments.

_____ 30. I give the members of the team lots of appreciation and support for their contributions.

Now, Turn to the Percentile Ranking

The Percentile Ranking page of your Feedback Report shows how your scores compare with those of others in our database.

- On what Practices are your percentile rankings between the 70th percentile and the 100th percentile? Between the 30th and the 70th? Between the 1st and 30th? Fill out the chart below.

Percentile	Model the Way	Inspire a Shared Vision	Challenge the Process	Enable Others to Act	Encourage the Heart
Below 30th					
30th to 70th					
70th to 100th					

- What do the percentile rankings tell you about your strengths and areas of improvement compared with other leaders?

_____

_____

_____

_____

_____

_____

_____

_____

_____

_____

Consider Feedback from Others

Now consider other feedback you have received and other observations you have.

- You may have received feedback on your leadership behavior from other sources—surveys, oral or written assessments from your manager, and interactions with others. If so, how does the LPI feedback compare to other feedback you've received? Where are the messages consistent, and where are there differences?

_____

_____

_____

_____

_____

_____

- What other observations about patterns and messages do you have right now? Write them down while they're fresh in your mind.

_____

_____

_____

_____

_____

_____

STEP 4

Seek Clarification

Sometimes you can't easily interpret and act on feedback you receive because you find it confusing. For instance, one person may rate you as doing something often, while another says you're doing it infrequently. The only way to deal with these situations is to identify confusing and contradictory messages and find a way to gain clarity about what's going on.

In other cases, you may simply not have enough information to make an informed decision. For example, you may have twelve direct reports, but have data from only three of them. You wonder whether these three direct reports are representative of all the others. You might want to ask for feedback from a few more direct reports in order to make better plans for your development.

- What data on your Feedback Report is confusing, incomplete, or contradictory?

_____

_____

_____

_____

_____

_____

- Can you think of some people who could help you clarify and interpret your feedback? Who are they and what would you ask them?

_____

_____

_____

_____

_____

_____

_____

_____

- What are some actions you could take to improve the quality of feedback you receive in the future?

_____

_____

_____

_____

_____

_____

_____

_____

STEP 5

Focus Your Developmental Efforts

If you want to be a better leader, you must work on *all* of The Five Practices of Exemplary Leadership. We recommend that you begin with the areas in which you need the most improvement—because it's often easiest to begin making improvements in areas that you don't engage in very frequently.

To improve your weak areas, use your strengths. For example, let's say that your lowest score is on Item #7, "Describes a compelling image of the future," and one of your highest scores is on Item #9, "Actively listens to diverse points of view." You could use your strength—active listening—to discover others' hopes, dreams, aspirations, favorite stories, and metaphors. By integrating their hopes and metaphors into your expression of a vision of the future, you can make it more compelling to others.

• Where would you most like to focus your efforts in improving your use of The Five Practices of Exemplary Leadership?

_____

_____

_____

_____

_____

_____

- Which Practice is your highest developmental priority, and which is the lowest? Order the Practices in terms of your developmental priorities, with one (1) being your highest priority and five (5) being your lowest.

    _____ Model the Way

    _____ Inspire a Shared Vision

    _____ Challenge the Process

    _____ Enable Others to Act

    _____ Encourage the Heart

- Take another look at the Leadership Behaviors Ranking page in your Feedback Report. On the Leadership Behaviors Organized by Practice on pages 11 and 12 of this Workbook, circle the three to five behaviors that represent your most immediate priorities.

STEP 6

Imagine Your Ideal Future Self

Given the Practices and the behaviors on which you want to focus your developmental efforts, imagine that you're executing them significantly more effectively than you are currently. Describe your ideal image of yourself with respect to these Practices and behaviors. Write a positive statement that describes the situation and the way you are behaving.

For instance, let's say you selected as one of your developmental areas, "I describe a compelling image of what our future could be like." Imagine yourself two years from now doing just that. You might write:

> "Whenever I talk about our company direction, people will comment on how positive and enthusiastic I am about our future. I will become more personally peaceful by not letting the little things I can't control detract me from the work; I will be realistic about facts but confident about possibilities, etc."

Or let's say you selected "I find ways to celebrate accomplishments." Imagine yourself one year from now doing that effortlessly. You might write:

> "I think about celebrating as an essential part of every project plan. I also pay close attention to times when people are working especially hard and spontaneously take a break for a picnic in the park, an afternoon at the movies, or some other gathering that will re-energize the group. People from other departments come to me for advice on celebrating accomplishments because they will see how effective I am. I keep a list of ideas for celebrations in my daily planner."

- Use the lines below to write a description of your ideal image of yourself:

_____

_____

_____

_____

_____

_____

_____

_____

_____

_____

_____

_____

_____

_____

_____

_____

_____

STEP 7

Overcome Barriers and Concerns

Before you can develop the best possible plan for improving as a leader, you not only need to understand the data, but you need to know what's inhibiting you from fully engaging in that behavior. Before you choose the actions you'll take to improve, it's essential to be honest with yourself about what's getting in your way of doing them *right now*. Maybe you aren't doing something right now because you didn't know it was important. Maybe you don't have the skills or haven't been trained to do it. Maybe you're resisting because you like being in charge, and you don't want to give up control.

- What gets in your way right now of achieving your ideal image? Check any of the following that might be creating barriers for you:

    _____ Lack of skills

    _____ Lack of training and development opportunities

    _____ Absence of a supportive manager or climate

    _____ Limited access to good role models

    _____ Few opportunities to take on challenging assignments

    _____ Fear of losing control of my team

    _____ Fear of being seen as weak

    _____ Fear that if I rock the boat it will be seen as a threat to the hierarchy

Other barriers:

_____

_____

_____

_____

_____

- What thoughts do you have about how you might overcome these barriers?

_____

_____

_____

_____

_____

_____

- How can you leverage and build on your strengths to overcome the barriers to make yourself an even better leader?

_____

_____

_____

_____

_____

STEP 8

Plan Next Steps

To achieve your ideal image of yourself as a leader, you need to take actions that will help you learn to lead. Our research, as well as that of others, indicates that there are three fundamental ways we learn to lead:

- *We learn from experience.* There's no substitute for learning by doing. Whether it's facilitating your team's meetings or leading a special project, the more chances you have to serve in leadership roles, the more likely it is that you'll develop the skills to lead—and the more likely that you'll learn the important leadership lessons that come only from the failures and successes of live action. What experiences do you need to have in order to achieve your ideal image?

_____

_____

_____

_____

_____

_____

_____

- *We learn by example.* Other people are excellent sources of guidance: Parents, teachers, neighbors, coaches, counselors, artisans, friends, co-workers, mentors, managers. Think about the people who've given you advice and support, filled you with curiosity, let you watch them while they worked, believed you had promise and inspired you to give your best, offered feedback about your behavior and its impact, and taught you the ropes. Who can serve as a positive role model to assist you in achieving your ideal image?

_____

_____

_____

_____

_____

_____

_____

_____

_____

_____

_____

_____

_____

_____

- *We learn in formal educational settings.* Training and other classroom opportunities can improve your chances of success. Studies show that the best leaders are the best learners—they don't pass up the chance to take a course when that's the best way to learn a skill. What formal training do you need in order to achieve your ideal image?

_____

_____

_____

_____

_____

_____

_____

_____

_____

_____

_____

_____

_____

_____

_____

The sample of a filled-out Leadership Development Worksheet and the blank worksheet that follows it are designed to help you select your strategy and plan specific action steps toward achieving your ideal.

LEADERSHIP DEVELOPMENT WORKSHEET
Sample

Today's Date: May 1, 2003

Leadership Development Period from May 1 to May 22, 2003

<u>Leadership Practice Focus:</u> *Inspire a Shared Vision*

Leadership Behavior Focus: *7. Describes a compelling image of the future*

Measurements of Progress: *I will know that I reached my improvement*
Turn your ideal image into *goal for the next three weeks when:*
measurable goals

- *I have written a 5 to 7 minute presentation of my vision*
- *My colleague, Terry, gives me feedback that he finds my statement "compelling"*
- *My direct reports give me feedback that my vision statement is at least a 3 on a scale of 1 (not at all compelling) to 5 (I'll sign up!)*

Primary Development Strategy:

Action Steps:

Circle one primary strategy from among these three basic approaches to learning and development:

Using your primary strategy, what actions do you need to take to achieve your ideal image—your measurable goals?

- (Experience)
- Example
- Education

- *Write a 5 to 7 minute vision statement*

- Make sure to include metaphors, examples, and other relevant imagery in my vision statement
- Sit down with Terry, who does this better than anyone I know, and share what I have written. Get his feedback. Make changes accordingly and review with him again.
- Present the vision statement to my team and ask for their honest feedback
- Revise again

Secondary Developmental Strategy:

- Experience
- Example
- (Education)

Action Steps:

- Listen to Martin Luther King, Jr.'s "I have a dream" speech and take notes on what he does to enlist others—his methods and content.
- Read chapter 6 in Jim Kouzes and Barry Posner's book, The Leadership Challenge on "Enlist Others."

LEADERSHIP DEVELOPMENT WORKSHEET

Today's Date: _____

Leadership Development Period from _____ **to** _____

Leadership Practice Focus: _____

Leadership Behavior Focus: _____

Measurements of Progress:
Turn your ideal image into
measurable goals

_____

_____

_____

_____

_____

_____

_____

_____

_____

_____

Primary Development
Strategy:

Circle one primary strategy
from among these three
basic approaches to
learning and development:

• Experience

• Example

• Education

Action Steps:

Using your primary strategy, what actions
do you need to take to achieve your ideal
image—your measurable goals?

_____

_____

_____

_____

_____

_____

_____

_____

_____

_____

_____

_____

_____

_____

_____

Secondary Developmental Strategy:

Circle a secondary strategy:

- **Experience**

- **Example**

- **Education**

Action Steps:

_____

_____

_____

_____

_____

_____

_____

_____

_____

STEP 9

Make a Public Commitment

Now it's time to go public with your commitments. From all the possibilities you've generated, select the critical few with which you want to start. These are not going to be the only things you do to become a better leader; these are just the actions you're going to take immediately and over the next few weeks. Learning to lead is a lifelong pursuit, and all we are asking for right now is a commitment to continuing your learning after this experience.

On page 33 is a "Commitment Memo" on which to record your initial commitments so that you can "go public" with them.

- First, pick a partner from among the people who've experienced this LPI Data Feedback Session with you. This is the person to whom you'll write the Commitment Memo and with whom you'll follow up in three weeks. (Make sure to pick your partner *before* you start to write to make sure everyone has a different partner.)

- Once you've made an agreement with one person to be one another's partner, take a few minutes to write down your near-term actions—ones that you'll take over the next three weeks.

- When you both have finished recording your commitments, get together and communicate what you're each going to do. Ask questions for clarification to make sure you understand one another's commitments.

- Make an agreement to get together in person or by phone. (Be sure to get a phone number and e-mail address.)

- Send your Commitment Memo to your partner so he or she has a copy to review before your meeting.

COMMITMENT MEMO

Today's Date: _____

To: [your partner] _____

From: _____

Re: My Leadership Development Actions

- To continue improving my capabilities as a leader, I commit to take the following actions over the next twenty-one days:

_____

_____

_____

_____

_____

_____

_____

- To get the process started, tomorrow morning I will take this first step:

_____

_____

_____

_____

Sign your name: _____

Phone number: _____

E-mail address: _____

STEP 10

Prepare to Share Your Feedback

There is one specific set of actions we highly recommend you take when you return to your organization. *We want you to share your LPI feedback.*

In completing the LPI process, you asked others to give you the gift of feedback about your leadership Practices. When people offer feedback, they'd like to know that you value this gift and that you intend to do something with it. We strongly encourage you to share your feedback with those who gave you this gift. There's a side benefit to sharing your feedback. When you're open about how you're perceived as a leader, you'll be acting on each of The Five Practices.

You can invite all those who gave you feedback to a group meeting, or you can schedule a one-on-one meeting with each person. In deciding which alternative to choose, consider your own comfort level, the norms of your organization, and the comfort level of those who gave you the feedback.

Here are a few tips that can help you:

- *Develop an agenda so that you can keep the meeting focused and on track.* Plan what you want to say and how you want to say it. Plan how you'll inform people and involve them.

- *Schedule the meeting.* It's best to share feedback in an organized fashion, so set up the group meeting or the individual sessions ahead of time.

- *Tell people what to expect.* At the beginning of the meeting, let people know how the meeting will be run, how long it will take, and what will be discussed.

- *Protect anonymity.* The people who gave you feedback assumed that their individual scores would remain anonymous. The only exception is your manager, if he or she completed an LPI-Observer form. So under no circumstances should you ask people to disclose the scores they gave you. Nor should people be pressured by others to disclose.

- *Express your gratitude.* Begin the discussion by saying "thank you." Let people know that you appreciate their feedback and their willingness to talk.

- *Describe the model.* Give a brief overview of The Five Practices. In order to fully describe the model, we recommend that you read *The Leadership Challenge* book.

- *Express your feelings.* Let people know how you feel about the feedback you received. By expressing your feelings, you will more easily establish trust.

- *Show your data.* If you're sharing your actual numbers (and we highly recommend that you do), either display them or distribute copies.

- *Talk about strengths (highest numbers).* Start with what you do well, according to the Observers. Cite specific examples: "My highest ratings were in the Practice of Enabling Others to Act. I think I demonstrated this Practice when I asked Leslie and Tom to give the annual report to the department heads instead of giving it myself. That's an example of Enabling." Ask people to share their own specific examples. Ask them how you can do even better.

- *Talk about opportunities for improvement (lowest numbers).* Define your understanding and perception of the feedback. Cite examples of instances in which you may not have done as well as you could. Ask others for specific examples. Then get feedback on how you can improve.

- *Discuss the Practice that shows the largest gap between your LPI-Self and LPI-Observer scores.* Ask people to help you understand why there's such a difference between your perceptions of yourself and their perceptions of you.

- *Express your appreciation.* Tell people how useful this meeting has been for you and encourage them to seek feedback on their own performance. Feedback is essential in improving what we do, whether it's leading, writing software code, serving a customer, or planting a tree. We all benefit from knowing how we're doing.

ABOUT THE AUTHORS

Jim Kouzes is chairman emeritus of the Tom Peters Company, a professional services firm which inspires organizations to invent the new world of work using leadership training and consulting solutions. He is also an Executive Fellow at the Center for Innovation and Entrepreneurship at the Leavey School of Business, Santa Clara University. **Barry Posner** is Dean of The Leavey School of Business and Professor of Leadership at Santa Clara University (Silicon Valley, California), where he has received numerous teaching and innovation awards, including his school's and his university's highest faculty awards. Jim and Barry were named by the International Management Council as the 2001 recipients of the prestigious Wilbur M. McFeely Award. This honor puts them in the company of Ken Blanchard, Stephen Covey, Peter Drucker, Edward Deming, Francis Hesselbein, Lee Iacocca, Rosabeth Moss Kanter, Norman Vincent Peale, and Tom Peters, previous recipients of the award.

In addition to their award-winning and best-selling book, *The Leadership Challenge: How to Keep Getting Extraordinary Things Done in Organizations,* Jim and Barry have co-authored *Credibility: How Leaders Gain It and Lose It, Why People Demand It* (2003), chosen by *Industry Week* as one of that year's five best management books, *Encouraging the Heart* (2003) and *The Leadership Challenge Planner* (1999). Jim and Barry also developed the highly acclaimed *Leadership Practices Inventory* (LPI), a 360-degree questionnaire assessing leadership behavior; the LPI is one of the most widely used leadership assessment instruments in the world. More than 150 doctoral dissertations and academic research projects have been based on the *Five Practices of Exemplary Leadership*™ model. CRM Learning has produced a number of leadership and management development videos based upon their publications.

Jim and Barry are frequent conference speakers and each has conducted leadership development programs for hundreds of organizations including: Alcoa, Applied Materials, ARCO, AT&T, Australia Post, Bank of America, Bose, Charles Schwab, Cisco Systems, Conference Board of Canada, Consumers Energy, Dell Computer, Deloitte Touche, Egon Zehnder International, Federal Express, Gymboree, Hewlett-Packard, IBM, Johnson & Johnson, Kaiser Foundation Health Plans and Hospitals, Lawrence Livermore

National Labs, Leadership Greater Hartford, Levi Strauss & Co., L. L. Bean, 3M, Merck, Mervyn's, Motorola, Network Appliance, Pacific Telesis, Roche Bioscience, Siemens, Sun Microsystems, TRW, Toyota, US Postal Service, United Way, and VISA.

Jim Kouzes is featured as one of workplace experts in George Dixon's book, *What Works at Work: Lessons from the Masters* (1988) and *in Learning Journeys: Top Management Experts Share Hard-Earned Lessons on Becoming Great Mentors and Leaders,* edited by Marshall Goldsmith, Beverly Kaye, and Ken Shelton (2000). Not only is he a highly regarded leadership scholar and an experienced executive, but *The Wall Street Journal* has cited him as one of the twelve most requested non-university executive education providers to U.S. companies. A popular seminar and conference speaker, Jim shares his insights about the leadership practices that contribute to high performance in individuals and organizations, and he leaves his audiences inspired with practical leadership tools and tips that they can apply at work, at home, and in their communities.

Jim directed the Executive Development Center (EDC) at Santa Clara University from 1981 through 1987. Under his leadership the EDC was awarded two gold medals from the Council for the Advancement and Support of Education. He also founded the Joint Center for Human Services Development at San Jose State University, which he managed from 1972 until 1980, and prior to that was on the staff of the University of Texas School of Social Work. His career in training and development began in 1969 when Jim, as part of the Southwest urban team, conducted seminars for Community Action Agency staff and volunteers in the "war on poverty" effort. Jim received his B. A. degree (1967) with honors from Michigan State University in political science and a certificate (1974) from San Jose State University's School of Business for completion of the internship in organization development.

Jim's interest in leadership began while he was growing up in Washington, D.C. In 1961 he was one of a dozen Eagle Scouts selected to serve in John F. Kennedy's Honor Guard at the presidential inauguration. Inspired by Kennedy, he served as a Peace Corps volunteer from 1967 through 1969. Jim can be reached at 408-978-1809 or jim@kouzesposner.com.

Barry Posner, an internationally renowned scholar and educator, is the author or coauthor of more than a hundred research and practitioner-focused articles in such publications as *Academy of Management Journal, Journal of Applied Psychology, Human Relations, Personnel Psychology, IEEE Transaction on Engineering Management, Journal of Business Ethics, California Management Review, Business Horizons,* and *Management Review.* In addition to his books with Jim Kouzes, he has coauthored several books on project management, most recently *Checkered Flag Projects: Ten Rules for Creating and Managing Projects That Win!* Barry is on the editorial review boards for the *Journal of Management Inquiry* and *Journal of Business Ethics.*

Barry received his B. A. degree (1970) with honors from the University of California, Santa Barbara, in political science. He received his M. A. degree (1972) from The Ohio State University in public administration and his Ph.D. degree (1976) from the

University of Massachusetts, Amherst, in organizational behavior and administrative theory. Having consulted with a wide variety of public and private sector organizations around the globe, Barry currently sits on the Board of Directors for the American Institute of Architects (AIA). He served previously on the boards of Public Allies, Big Brothers/Big Sisters of Santa Clara County, the Center for Excellence in Non-Profits, Sigma Phi Epsilon Fraternity, and several start-up companies. At Santa Clara University he has previously served as Associate Dean for Graduate Programs and Managing Partner for the Executive Development Center.

Barry's interest in leadership began as a student during the turbulent unrest on college campuses in the late 1960s, when he was participating and reflecting on the balance between energetic collective action and chaotic and frustrated anarchy. At one time, he aspired to be a Supreme Court justice, but realizing he would have to study law, he redirected his energies into understanding people, organizational systems, and the liberation of the human spirit. Barry can be reached at (408) 554-4523 or bposner@scu.edu.

More information about Jim and Barry, and their work, can be found at their Web site: www.theleadershipchallenge.com.

STUDENT LEADERSHIP PRACTICES INVENTORY – SELF

How frequently do you *typically* engage in the following behaviors and actions?
Circle the number to the right of each statement, using the scale below, that best applies.

1	2	3	4	5
RARELY OR SELDOM	**ONCE IN A WHILE**	**SOMETIMES**	**VERY OFTEN**	**FREQUENTLY**

1. I set a personal example of what I expect from other people.	1	2	3	4	5
2. I look ahead and communicate about what I believe will affect us in the future.	1	2	3	4	5
3. I look around for ways to develop and challenge my skills and abilities.	1	2	3	4	5
4. I foster cooperative rather than competitive relationships among people I work with.	1	2	3	4	5
5. I praise people for a job well done.	1	2	3	4	5
6. I spend time and energy making sure that people in our organization adhere to the principles and standards we have agreed upon.	1	2	3	4	5
7. I describe to others in our organization what we should be capable of accomplishing.	1	2	3	4	5
8. I look for ways that others can try out new ideas and methods.	1	2	3	4	5
9. I actively listen to diverse points of view.	1	2	3	4	5
10. I encourage others as they work on activities and programs in our organization.	1	2	3	4	5
11. I follow through on the promises and commitments I make in this organization.	1	2	3	4	5
12. I talk with others about sharing a vision of how much better the organization could be in the future.	1	2	3	4	5
13. I keep current on events and activities that might affect our organization.	1	2	3	4	5
14. I treat others with dignity and respect.	1	2	3	4	5
15. I give people in our organization support and express appreciation for their contributions.	1	2	3	4	5

STUDENT LEADERSHIP PRACTICES INVENTORY – SELF

Your Name: _____

Instructions

On the next two pages are thirty statements describing various leadership behaviors. Please read each statement carefully. Then rate *yourself* in terms of *how frequently* you engage in the behavior described. *This is not a test* (there are no right or wrong answers). The usefulness of the feedback from this inventory will depend on how honest you are with yourself and how frequently you *actually* engage in each of these behaviors.

Consider each statement in the context of one student organization with which you are now (or have been most) involved with. This organization could be a club, team, chapter, group, unit, hall, program, project, and the like. As you respond to each statement, maintain a consistent perspective to your particular organization. The rating scale provides five choices. Circle the number that best applies to each statement:

(1) If you RARELY or SELDOM do what is described
(2) If you do what is described ONCE IN A WHILE
(3) If you SOMETIMES do what is described
(4) If you OFTEN do what is described
(5) If you VERY FREQUENTLY or ALMOST ALWAYS
    do what is described

In selecting the response, be realistic about the extent to which you *actually* engage in the behavior. Do *not* answer in terms of how you would like to see yourself or in terms of what you should be doing. Answer in terms of how you *typically* behave.

For example, the first statement is "I set a personal example of what I expect from other people." If you believe you do this *once in a while,* circle the number 2. If you believe you do this *often,* circle the number 4. Select and circle only one option (response number) for each statement.

Please respond to every statement. If you can't respond to a statement (or feel that it doesn't apply), circle a 1. When you have responded to all thirty statements, please turn to the response sheet on the back page and transfer your responses as instructed.

1	2	3	4	5
RARELY OR SELDOM	ONCE IN A WHILE	SOMETIMES	VERY OFTEN	FREQUENTLY

16. I find ways to get feedback about how my actions affect other people's performance.　　1　2　3　4　5

17. I talk with others about how their own interests can be met by working toward a common goal.　　1　2　3　4　5

18. When things do not go as we expected, I ask, "What can we learn from this experience?"　　1　2　3　4　5

19. I support the decisions that other people in our organization make on their own.　　1　2　3　4　5

20. I make it a point to publicly recognize people who show commitment to our values.　　1　2　3　4　5

21. I build consensus on an agreed-upon set of values for our organization.　　1　2　3　4　5

22. I am upbeat and positive when talking about what our organization aspires to accomplish.　　1　2　3　4　5

23. I make sure that we set goals and make specific plans for the projects we undertake.　　1　2　3　4　5

24. I give others a great deal of freedom and choice in deciding how to do their work.　　1　2　3　4　5

25. I find ways for us to celebrate accomplishments.　　1　2　3　4　5

26. I talk about the values and principles that guide my actions.　　1　2　3　4　5

27. I speak with conviction about the higher purpose and meaning of what we are doing.　　1　2　3　4　5

28. I take initiative in experimenting with the way we can do things in our organization.　　1　2　3　4　5

29. I provide opportunities for others to take on leadership responsibilities.　　1　2　3　4　5

30. I make sure that people in our organization are creatively recognized for their contributions.　　1　2　3　4　5

Transferring the Responses

After you have responded to the thirty statements on the previous two pages, please transfer your responses to the blanks below. This will make it easier to record and score your responses.

Notice that the numbers of the statements are listed *horizontally* across the page. Make sure that the number you assigned to each statement is transferred to the appropriate blank. Remember to fill in a response option (1, 2, 3, 4, 5) for every statement.

1. _____	2. _____	3. _____	4. _____	5. _____
6. _____	7. _____	8. _____	9. _____	10. _____
11. _____	12. _____	13. _____	14. _____	15. _____
16. _____	17. _____	18. _____	19. _____	20. _____
21. _____	22. _____	23. _____	24. _____	25. _____
26. _____	27. _____	28. _____	29. _____	30. _____

Further Instructions

Please write your name here: _____

You should have received instructions to:

☐ Bring this page with you to the class (seminar or workshop) or
☐ Return this form to:

_____

_____

_____

If you are interested in feedback from other people, ask them to complete the *Student LPI-Observer*. This form provides perspectives on your leadership behaviors as perceived by other people.

Copyright © 2006 by James M. Kouzes and Barry Z. Posner. All rights reserved.

Published by Jossey-Bass

A Wiley Imprint
989 Market Street, San Francisco, CA 94103-1741   www.josseybass.com

No part of this publication may be reproduced, stored in a retrieval system, or transmitted in any form or by any means, electronic, mechanical, photocopying, recording, scanning, or otherwise, except as permitted under Section 107 or 108 of the 1976 United States Copyright Act, without either the prior written permission of the publisher, or authorization through payment of the appropriate per-copy fee to the Copyright Clearance Center, Inc., 222 Rosewood Drive, Danvers, MA 01923, 978-750-8400, fax 978-646-8600, or on the Web at www.copyright.com. Requests to the publisher for permission should be addressed to the Permissions Department, John Wiley & Sons, Inc., 111 River Street, Hoboken, NJ 07030, 201-748-6011, fax 201-748-6008, or online at http://www.wiley.com/go/permissions.

Jossey-Bass books and products are available through most bookstores. To contact Jossey-Bass directly call our Customer Care Department within the U.S. at 800-956-7739, outside the U.S. at 317-572-3986, or fax 317-572-4002.

ISBN:0-7879-8020-X

Printed in the United States of America

10 9 8 7 6

ISBN 978-0-7879-8020-7
90000